Toy Poodle

Oodles of Fun

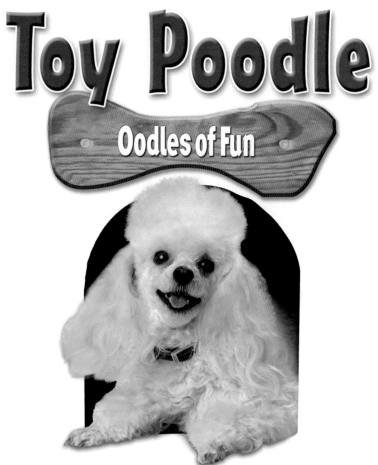

by Meish Goldish

Consultant: Del Dahl
Author of *The Complete Poodle*
Member of the Board of Directors of
the Poodle Club of America

BEARPORT
PUBLISHING

New York, New York

Credits

Cover and Title Page, © Ardea/Retna Ltd.; TOC, © Chin Kit Sen/Shutterstock; 4, Courtesy of Sharon Robinson; 5, Courtesy of Sharon Robinson; 6, Courtesy of Sharon Robinson; 7, Courtesy of Sharon Robinson; 8, © Dale C. Spartas/Corbis; 9T, © Chip Laughton/Windigo Images; 9B, © Dale C. Spartas/Corbis; 10, © F. Boucher, Das gelehrige Huendchen Boucher, Francois 1703-1770. 'Das gelehrige Huendchen' (La Gimblette), um 1740. Pendant zu 'L'enfant gate' (Das verzo- gene Kind). Oel auf Leinwand, 52,5 x 41,5 cm. Inv.Nr. 2468 Karlsruhe, Staatliche Kunstha/akg-images; 11L, © Paul Hilton/epa/Corbis; 11R, © Peter Young/fotoLibra; 12T, © Juniors Bildarchiv/Alamy; 12C, © Mark Raycroft/Minden Pictures; 12B, © Paulette Johnson; 13, © Jean Michel Labat/Ardea; 14, © Yves Lanceau/NHPA/Photoshot; 15T, © Omar Torres/AFP Photo/Newscom; 15B, © Ralph Reinhold/Animals Animals Enterprises; 16, © Juniors Bildarchiv/Alamy; 17T, Courtesy of Beth Franklin/Hand-In-Paw; 17B, © Nancy George-Michalson and Callie; 18, © O. Diez/Arco Images/Alamy; 19, © Yuriko Nakao/Reuters/Landov; 20, © Paulette Johnson; 21, © Ron Kimball/kimballstock; 22T, © Connie Halcom/Rainbow Toy Poodles; 22B, © Connie Halcom/Rainbow Toy Poodles; 23, © Eriko Sugita/Reuters/Landov; 24, © AP Images/Richmond Times-Dispatch, Rex Bowman; 25, © Los Angeles Times Photo by Lawrence K. Ho, 2008, reprinted with permission; 26, © Dianna Jones; 27, © Omar Torres/AFP/Getty Images; 28, © Yoshio Tomii/SuperStock; 29, © Omar Torres/AFP Photo/Newscom; 31, © Rhonda O'Donnell/Shutterstock; 32, © Chin Kit Sen/Shutterstock.

Publisher: Kenn Goin
Editorial Director: Adam Siegel
Creative Director: Spencer Brinker
Photo Researcher: Daniella Nilva
Design: Dawn Beard Creative

Library of Congress Cataloging-in-Publication Data

Goldish, Meish.
  Toy poodle : oodles of fun / by Meish Goldish.
     p. cm. — (Little dogs rock!)
  Includes bibliographical references and index.
  ISBN-13: 978-1-59716-746-8 (library binding)
  ISBN-10: 1-59716-746-0 (library binding)
  1. Toy poodle—Juvenile literature. I. Title.
  SF429.M57G65 2009
  636.76—dc22
                        2008039891

For more information, write to Bearport Publishing Company, Inc., 101 Fifth Avenue, Suite 6R, New York, New York 10003. Printed in the United States of America.

10 9 8 7 6 5 4 3 2 1

Contents

Tops in Tricks 4

Sharing the Fun...................... 6

Water Dogs 8

Down-Sizing 10

Measuring Up 12

Getting Clipped..................... 14

Toy Joy 16

Popular Pets........................ 18

Tiny Tips 20

Toy Puppies........................ 22

A Small Hero 24

Little Champs 26

Toy Poodles at a Glance............... 28

Best in Show......................... 29

Glossary............................ 30

Bibliography 31

Read More 31

Learn More Online................... 31

Index 32

About the Author.................... 32

Tops in Tricks

Sharon Robinson couldn't believe how smart her new toy poodle was. The seven-and-a-half-week-old puppy, named Chanda-Leah, quickly learned simple **commands** such as *sit, stay, lie down,* and *roll over.* Yet that was only the beginning.

Sharon Robinson of Ontario, Canada, began to train Chanda-Leah in 1994.

By the age of five, the toy poodle had learned to perform more than 500 tricks. When Chanda-Leah had to go to the bathroom, she would ring the bell in her crate to let Sharon know it was time to let her out. The tiny dog smiled and sneezed on **cue**. She untied knots and painted pictures. She even added, subtracted, and multiplied numbers.

Chanda-Leah was listed in *The Guinness Book of World Records* four times between 1999 and 2003 for being able to perform more tricks than any other dog.

▲ Chanda-Leah's paintings became popular collectors' items.

Sharing the Fun

Chanda-Leah's **intelligence** and talent for performing tricks made her a **celebrity**. The toy poodle appeared on national television shows. She received letters, phone calls, and e-mails from many famous people, including the queen of England. Yet Sharon wanted ordinary people to enjoy Chanda-Leah's talents, too.

Chanda-Leah learned to climb on her skateboard and push it along.

Sharon believed that the little dog could "brighten up people's lives." So Sharon and Chanda-Leah visited schools, nursing homes, and hospitals. The tiny poodle amazed audiences with her tricks. She balanced a cup on her head and a cookie on her nose—at the same time! She even played the piano. Throughout her life, this toy poodle brought oodles of fun to thousands of children and adults!

Dr. Stanley Coren, a dog **expert**, rates the poodle as the second most intelligent kind of dog. The border collie is rated first.

▲ **Chanda-Leah played the piano, as well as the drums and saxophone.**

Water Dogs

Toy poodles like Chanda-Leah have always been known for their intelligence. Yet the little animals are a fairly new kind of dog. Hundreds of years ago, there were no small poodles—only large ones, which are now called standard poodles. These big, curly-haired dogs were used by hunters in Germany as early as the 1300s.

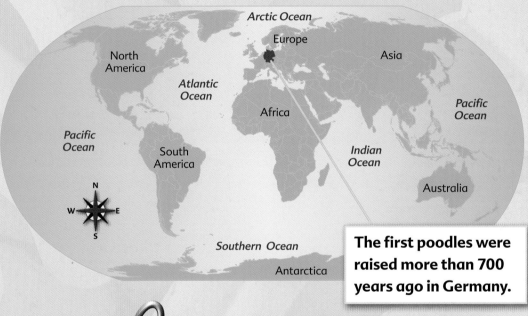

Arctic Ocean

Europe

North America

Asia

Atlantic Ocean

Pacific Ocean

Africa

Pacific Ocean

South America

Indian Ocean

Australia

N
W E
S

Southern Ocean

Antarctica

The first poodles were raised more than 700 years ago in Germany.

Drawings of curly-haired poodle-like dogs have been found on Greek and Roman coins that are about 2,000 years old. It is believed that today's poodle is related to these **ancient** dogs.

▲ **Poodles are still used by hunters today.**

The name *poodle* actually comes from a German word—*pudelin*. It means "to splash in the water." Poodles in Germany swam in lakes and rivers to collect birds shot by hunters. Later, poodles became popular hunting dogs in France as well. The poodle was admired so much in that country that it was named the national dog of France.

▲ This poodle races through the water to collect a duck shot by a hunter.

◄ A poodle bringing a duck back to a hunter

Down-Sizing

Not everyone in France needed a big hunting dog. Some people wanted a smaller-sized poodle as a pet. So dog owners began **breeding** small standard poodles with other small standards. Over time, the result was a smaller kind of poodle, called the miniature. By the 1600s, small miniature poodles were bred with one another to create an even smaller kind of poodle—the toy poodle.

This painting from around ▶ 1740 shows a French woman with her toy poodle. The little dogs were so popular in France that they were often called French poodles. Many people still use that term today.

Toy poodles quickly grew popular in France. Many rich people kept them as house pets. The tiny dog sat comfortably on an owner's lap and it was easy to carry around. The dog's popularity soon spread to Spain, England, and finally, in the 1800s, to the United States.

▲ **Toy poodles and other small dogs that can sit on a person's lap are called lapdogs.**

Large and small poodles were popular circus performers in the 1800s—and still are today. They are able to quickly learn many tricks due to their great intelligence.

Measuring Up

The **American Kennel Club** (AKC) is an organization that keeps records of the different kinds of dogs bred in the United States. As large and small poodles from Europe found homes across America in the early 1900s, the AKC officially recognized three different sizes of poodles.

◀ **Standard poodles**

Miniature poodles ▶

◀ **Toy poodles**

The *standard poodle,* which is the largest size, is any poodle more than 15 inches (38 cm) high at the shoulders. The next in line is the *miniature poodle.* It is more than 10 inches (25.4 cm) tall but less than 15 inches (38 cm). The *toy poodle,* which is the smallest, must be 10 inches (25.4 cm) or shorter.

At first, the AKC counted toy poodles as a different **breed** of dog because of their tiny size. In 1943, however, all three sizes were considered to be one breed since they all have the same **physical** shape.

▲ **A standard poodle (left), a miniature poodle (center), and a toy poodle (right)**

Getting Clipped

Toy poodles are known for their tiny size. Yet they are also known for their unusual haircuts. Many poodle owners shave off parts of their dogs' hair. The result is the famous poodle clip. How did this hairstyle come about?

A corded poodle

Some poodle owners twist their dogs' hair into ropes called "cords." Although corded **coats** are not common today, they were very popular in England during the 1800s.

Hundreds of years ago, hunters shaved the legs and rear part of their large poodles. Removing the hair helped the dogs swim more easily. The rest of the hair was left on the hunting dog's body to keep its head, chest, and **joints** warm in the cold, icy water. Today, some toy poodle owners copy this hairstyle for their dogs' coats.

A poodle's haircut ▶ can give the dog a fancy look.

◀ Some owners don't give their dogs a fancy poodle clip.

Toy Joy

Toy poodles don't just have great haircuts. They also have great faces. Some owners say their dogs look like they are smiling when their lips curl up at the corners. In fact, the tiny dogs are happiest when they are around people.

▲ **A poodle often seems to wear a smile on its face.**

Toy poodles are very good at being able to **sense** when someone is happy or sad. They easily notice changes in a person's tone of voice or **body language**.

Toy poodles love attention from children and adults. As a result, some of them are used as **therapy dogs**. The happy little dogs visit children and adults in schools, hospitals, and nursing homes. They do a great job of cheering up people who are sad, lonely, or sick.

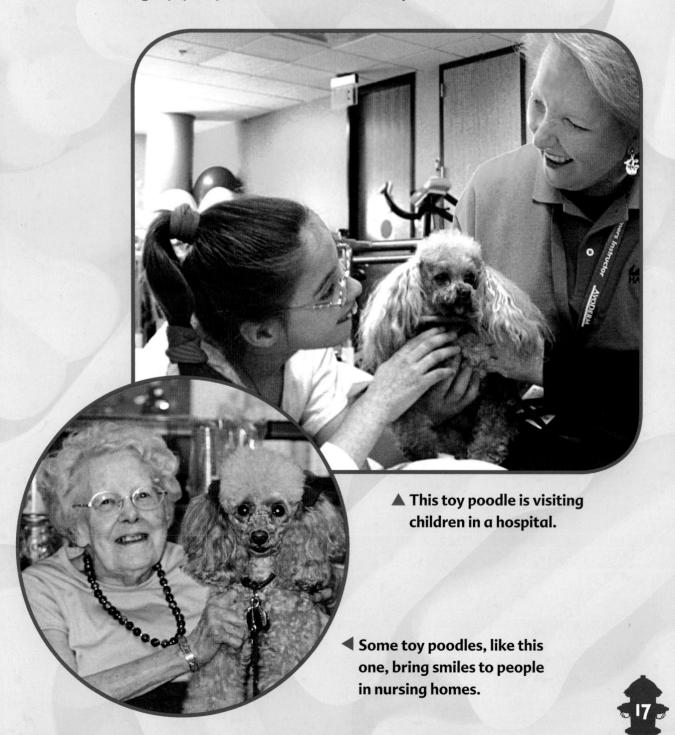

▲ This toy poodle is visiting children in a hospital.

◀ Some toy poodles, like this one, bring smiles to people in nursing homes.

Popular Pets

The cheerful personality of toy poodles has made them popular pets—and so has their tiny size. Since they are so small, the little dogs can get enough exercise living in a small city apartment or a large house in the country.

A toy poodle's small size makes it easy for people who travel a lot to take the little dog with them wherever they go.

Many people also love toy poodles because they are smart and easy to train. Toy poodles quickly learn how to pick up their own toys or **fetch** items from other rooms.

Their coats are a plus for many owners, too. Although poodles are hairy, they don't **shed**. As a result, they don't leave their fur around the house. This makes them great pets for people who are allergic to the bits of skin and oil in dog hair.

Although poodles don't shed, owners still need to regularly brush their dogs' coats so that the curly fur doesn't become knotted.

Tiny Tips

Toy poodles are popular pets, yet they're not for everyone. A family with young children should not own a toy poodle. These small dogs are **fragile** and must be handled gently. A young child might hold or hug a toy poodle too roughly, without knowing it.

Children need to be taught how to handle toy poodles so that the tiny dogs don't get hurt.

Toy poodles also demand a lot of attention from their owners. The dogs don't like to be ignored or left alone. So owners must be ready to spend lots of time with their little friends. In return, they will get hours and hours of love.

Toy poodles have a good memory. As a result, owners need to be **consistent** when teaching them. A poodle that is allowed to lie on furniture once may not understand if it is not allowed to jump up another time—and it can get upset.

Toy Puppies

Toy poodles are tiny as adults. Imagine, then, how tiny a baby toy poodle is! At birth, it weighs only about 1.5 to 4.5 ounces (42.5 to 127.5 g)—less than a baseball. A puppy may be bigger if it's the only one in the **litter**. However, most toy poodle litters have three or four puppies in them.

◀ A baby toy poodle doubles its weight each week during the first month of its life.

A toy poodle puppy ▶ drinks its mother's milk for the first eight weeks of its life.

In recent years, some dog breeders have been producing very tiny toy poodles. They are called teacup poodles. Their extra-small size often leads to serious health problems. Some teacup poodles have very short lives—only three to five years. Many dog experts advise pet owners not to buy teacup poodles.

A three-week-old teacup poodle puppy

An adult teacup poodle weighs only 2.5 to 4 pounds (1.1 to 1.8 kg).

A Small Hero

Poodle puppies require special care and love. Jana Kohl knows that well. When she wanted to buy a baby toy poodle, she visited a **puppy mill** in Texas. The dogs there are raised and sold to pet stores. To her horror, she found hundreds of puppies at the mill that were locked in small, dirty cages. They didn't get any sunlight or exercise.

There are thousands of puppy mills in the United States. They sell their dogs to pet stores around the country. To avoid buying puppies from a mill, a person should go directly to a dog breeder or animal shelter.

▲ **These dogs were rescued from a puppy mill in Virginia.**

Jana left the mill in shock. Yet she also left with a goal—to let people know about the horrible conditions in puppy mills. A few months later Jana **adopted** an adult toy poodle, Baby. She had been rescued from a puppy mill. Today, Jana and Baby travel across the country, educating people about these cruel places. Jana hopes to get laws passed that will make puppy mills **illegal**.

▲ **Jana Kohl (right) wrote a book about her experiences with Baby (left). Baby has only three legs due to her mistreatment when she was in a puppy mill.**

Little Champs

Toy poodles may be small, yet the tiny dogs have made a big name for themselves. In 2001, Hollywood star Jennifer Lopez carried a toy poodle named Cash onstage at the 28th Annual American Music Awards. Millions of TV viewers around the world got to see just how cute a toy poodle can be.

Cash

In 2007, Smash JP Talk About, a toy poodle from Japan, won the **Best in Show** award at the World Dog Show in Mexico City. He beat out 5,000 other dogs in the **competition**. They represented about 300 different breeds. Smash proved that toy poodles really are giants in the world of little dogs!

The poodle is one of the top ten most popular dog breeds in the United States.

▲ **Smash JP Talk About after winning his award at the World Dog Show**

Toy Poodles at a Glance

Weight:	4 to 6 pounds (1.8 to 2.7 kg)
Height at Shoulder:	10 inches (25.4 cm) or shorter
Coat:	Thick, curly; doesn't shed
Colors:	White, red, black, gray, silver, brown, light brown, apricot, cream, blue
Country of Origin:	Germany
Life Span:	14–16 years
Personality:	Lively, happy, playful, loving, loyal; likes attention; jumps and barks a lot

Best in Show

What makes a great toy poodle? Every owner knows that his or her dog is special. Judges in dog shows, however, look very carefully at a toy poodle's appearance and behavior. Here are some of the things they look for:

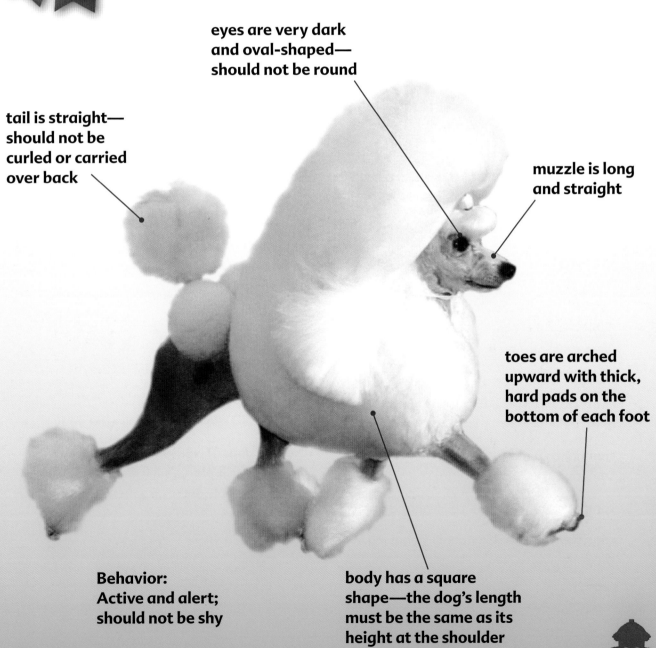

eyes are very dark and oval-shaped— should not be round

tail is straight— should not be curled or carried over back

muzzle is long and straight

toes are arched upward with thick, hard pads on the bottom of each foot

Behavior: Active and alert; should not be shy

body has a square shape—the dog's length must be the same as its height at the shoulder

Glossary

adopted (uh-DOPT-id) taken in as part of one's family

American Kennel Club (uh-MER-i-kuhn KEN-uhl KLUHB) a national organization that is involved in many activities having to do with dogs, including collecting information about dog breeds, registering purebred dogs, and setting rules for dog shows

ancient (AYN-shunt) very old

Best in Show (BEST IN SHOH) the top-rated dog in a dog show

body language (BOD-ee LANG-wij) a message suggested by the way a person sits, stands, or moves his or her body

breed (BREED) a kind of dog

breeding (BREED-ing) keeping animals with special characteristics so that they can mate and produce offspring with those same characteristics

celebrity (suh-LEB-ruh-*tee*) a famous person or animal

coats (KOHTS) the fur on dogs or other animals

commands (kuh-MANDZ) orders given by someone

competition (*kom*-puh-TISH-uhn) a contest

consistent (kuhn-SISS-tuhnt) behaving in the same way

cue (KYOO) a signal to do something

expert (EK-spurt) someone who knows a lot about a subject

fetch (FECH) to go after and bring back something

fragile (FRAJ-il) weak; easily hurt or broken

illegal (i-LEE-guhl) against the law

intelligence (in-TEL-uh-juntss) the ability to understand, solve problems, and learn

joints (JOINTS) places in the body where two bones meet

litter (LIT-ur) a group of baby animals, such as puppies or kittens, that are born to the same mother at the same time

physical (FIZ-uh-kuhl) having to do with the body

puppy mill (PUHP-ee MIL) a place where large numbers of dogs are raised to be sold, but are poorly cared for

sense (SENSS) to feel or be aware of something

shed (SHED) to have hair fall off a body

therapy dogs (THER-uh-pee DAWGZ) dogs that visit places such as hospitals to cheer up people and make them feel more comfortable

Bibliography

Biniok, Janice. *The Poodle (Our Best Friends).* Pittsburgh, PA: Eldorado Ink (2008).

Fernandez, Amy. *Poodles (Animal Planet Pet Care Library).* Neptune City, NJ: T.F.H. Publications (2008).

Stahlkuppe, Joe. *Poodles: Everything About Purchase, Care, Nutrition, Behavior, and Training.* Hauppauge, NY: Barron's (2007).

Read More

Schuh, Mari. *Poodles.* Minneapolis, MN: Bellwether Media (2009).

Stone, Lynn M. *Poodles.* Vero Beach, FL: Rourke (2003).

Trumbauer, Lisa. *Poodles.* Mankato, MN: Capstone Press (2006).

Learn More Online

To learn more about toy poodles, visit
www.bearportpublishing.com/LittleDogsRock

Index

American Kennel Club (AKC) 12–13

Baby 25

Cash 26
Chanda-Leah 4–5, 6–7, 8
circus 11
coats 14–15, 19, 28
colors 28
Coren, Dr. Stanley 7

exercise 18, 24

France 9, 10–11

Germany 8–9, 28
Guinness Book of World Records, The 5

haircuts 14–15, 16
height 13, 28–29
hunting 8–9, 10, 15

Kohl, Jana 24–25

life span 28
Lopez, Jennifer 26

miniature poodle 10, 12–13

personality 16–17, 18, 28–29
poodle clip 14–15
puppies 22–23, 24
puppy mills 24–25

Robinson, Sharon 4–5, 6–7

shedding 19, 28
Smash JP Talk About 27
standard poodle 8, 10, 12–13

teacup poodles 23
therapy dogs 17
training 19, 21

weight 22–23, 28
World Dog Show 27

About the Author

Meish Goldish has written more than 100 books for children. His book *Dogs (Smart Animals!)* was a Children's Choices selection in 2008. He lives in Brooklyn, New York.